Delicious
pastries

Delicious
pastries

Love Food ™ is an imprint of Parragon Books Ltd

Parragon
Queen Street House
4 Queen Street
Bath BA1 1HE

Cover and internal design by Mark Cavanagh
Introduction by Bridget Jones
Photography by Günter Beer
Additional photography by Mike Cooper
Home Economist Stevan Paul

ISBN 978-1-4054-9642-1
Printed in China

Notes for the reader
• This book uses metric and imperial measurements. Follow the same units of
measurement throughout; do not mix imperial and metric.
• All spoon measurements are level: teaspoons are assumed to be 5 ml, and
tablespoons are assumed to be 15 ml.
• Unless otherwise stated, milk is assumed to be low fat and eggs are medium. The
times given are an approximate guide only.
• Some recipes contain nuts. If you are allergic to nuts you should avoid using them
and any products containing nuts. Recipes using raw or very lightly cooked eggs
should be avoided by infants, the elderly, pregnant women, convalescents and anyone
suffering from illness.

Contents

Pastries

Pastry chef superiority should not deter anyone from trying basic pastry-making methods. Getting it right is no mystery, but a matter of a few general guidelines with the right technique for the right dough.

• Cool ingredients, hands, equipment and workplace suit pastry making.

• Allow chilling time when necessary – it makes the difference between unmanageable dough and roll-easy results.

• Practise a light touch to avoid tough dough. Use fingertips not palms to rub fat into flour. A food processor is brilliant for rubbing fat into flour and kneading Danish pastry dough.

• There is no need to grease tins unless the recipe specifically advises you to do so.

• Most pastries benefit from being cooked at high temperature, at least at first.

Fantastic filo

Buy filo from a shop that has a good turnover (old stock tends to be brittle).

• Cover filo with clingfilm or a damp cloth when not actually in use as the sheets dry quickly and become brittle.

• Brush filo with fat to make the edges stick together and to keep the layers crisp and separate. A little oil works but melted butter is traditional: a mix of butter melted in oil works well too.

Perfect puff and Danish pastries

Keeping everything well chilled is vital for success. Chill between rollings, allowing time for the dough to rest. Danish, especially, has to be left overnight before finally rolling out and shaping.

• Bake puff pastry at a high temperature for the layers to rise and separate.

• Rinse baking tins in cold water or put a shallow tin of boiling water in the bottom of the oven to give a good rise.
• Brush puff and Danish pastry with egg or milk to glaze; egg white and sugar make a sweet glaze for sweet pastries.

Simply choux

Choux pastry is so simple to make; it is just a case of using the right method at the right time.
• Melt the butter in the water slowly, without boiling until the fat has melted, then quickly bring to a boil.
• Add the flour (always plain) all at once before removing the pan from the heat and stirring immediately. Stir until the mixture comes away from the pan but do not beat or it will become greasy.
• Leave the paste to cool slightly before adding the eggs.

• Beat in the eggs. An electric beater is useful for this. Continue beating until the mixture is smooth and glossy.
• Split cooked choux pastries immediately after removing them from the oven to allow the steam to escape and keep the outside crisp. The inside should be slightly sticky.

So short

Short pastries are crumbly and crisp – a combination of fat and flour with a little liquid. Too much water will make the dough tough, as will heavy handling.
• A high proportion of fat makes rich, very short pastry – the usual amount is half fat to flour or three-quarters fat to flour for rich short pastries.
• Butter gives the best flavour; lard or white fat makes the mixture very short. The classic combination is half and half of each.

Perfect Puff

apple danish

makes 16

for the Danish pastry dough

275 g/10 oz strong white flour, plus extra for dusting

175 g/6 oz butter, well chilled, plus extra for greasing

1/4 tsp salt

7 g/1/4 oz easy-blend dried yeast

2 tbsp caster sugar

1 egg, at room temperature

1 tsp vanilla extract

6 tbsp lukewarm water

milk, for glazing

for the filling

2 cooking apples, peeled, cored and chopped

grated rind of 1 lemon

4 tbsp sugar

Place the flour in a bowl and rub in 25 g/1 oz of the butter. Set aside. Chill the remaining butter in the freezer until hard but not frozen. Dust with flour and grate coarsely into a bowl. Chill.

Stir the salt, yeast and sugar into the flour mixture. In another bowl, beat the egg with the vanilla extract and water, then add to the flour and mix to form a dough. Knead the dough for 10 minutes on a floured surface, then chill for 10 minutes.

Roll out the dough to 30 x 20 cm/12 x 8 inches and mark it lengthways into thirds. Sprinkle the grated butter evenly over the top two-thirds, leaving a 1–2-cm/1/2–3/4-inch border around the edge, and press down lightly.

Fold the bottom third of dough over the centre, then fold the top third down. Press the edges of the dough with a rolling pin and give it a quarter-turn (so the short edge is nearest you). Roll out as big as the original rectangle. Fold the bottom third up and the top third down again. Press the edges. Wrap in clingfilm and chill for 30 minutes. Repeat this rolling, folding and turning four times, chilling well each time. Finally, chill the dough overnight.

Preheat the oven to 200°C/400°F/Gas Mark 6. Grease two baking sheets. For the filling, mix the apples with the lemon rind and 3 tablespoons of the sugar. Roll out the dough into a 40-cm/16-inch square and cut into 16 squares. Pile a little of the apple filling in the centre of each square, reserving any juice to glaze. Brush the edges with milk and fold the corners together into the centre over the filling. Place on the baking sheets and chill for about 15 minutes.

Brush the pastries with the reserved juice and sprinkle with the remaining sugar. Bake for 10 minutes. Reduce the oven temperature to 180°C/350°F/Gas Mark 4 and bake for a further 10–15 minutes, until browned.

makes 16

for the Danish pastry dough

275 g/10 oz strong white flour, plus extra for dusting

175 g/6 oz butter, well chilled, plus extra for greasing

1/4 tsp salt

7 g/1/4 oz easy-blend dried yeast

2 tbsp caster sugar

1 egg, at room temperature

1 tsp vanilla extract

6 tbsp lukewarm water

beaten egg or milk, for glazing

for the filling

115 g/4 oz ground almonds

4 tbsp caster sugar

1 egg, beaten

a few drops of almond essence

16 glacé cherries

for the icing

115 g/4 oz icing sugar

a little water

cherry & almond windmills

For the Danish pastry dough, follow the instructions on page 11 as far as the final rolling, folding and chilling stage.

Once the dough has chilled for several hours or overnight, prepare the filling. Mix together the almonds and sugar, then stir in the egg with a few drops of almond essence to make a paste. Divide the paste into 16 portions and roll them into balls.

Grease two baking sheets. Roll out the dough into a 40-cm/16-inch square and cut into 16 squares. For each square of dough, make a diagonal cut in from each corner, just over halfway towards the middle. Place a ball of almond paste in the centre. Fold alternate corners to the middle, pressing them into the paste. Top with a cherry and place on a baking sheet. Chill for 15 minutes.

Meanwhile, preheat the oven to 200°C/400°F/Gas Mark 6. Brush the windmills with a little beaten egg or milk and bake for 10 minutes. Reduce the temperature to 180°C/350°F/Gas Mark 4 and bake for a further 5–10 minutes, until browned.

For the icing, place the icing sugar in a bowl and mix in a little water. Drizzle the icing over the pastries as soon as they come out of the oven. Transfer to a wire rack and leave to cool completely.

makes 8

250 g/9 oz ready-made puff pastry

milk, for glazing

for the filling

450 g/1 lb cooking apples, peeled, cored and chopped

grated rind of 1 lemon (optional)

pinch of ground cloves (optional)

3 tbsp sugar

for the orange sugar

1 tbsp sugar, for sprinkling

finely grated rind of 1 orange

for the orange cream

250 ml/8 fl oz double cream

grated rind of 1 orange and juice of ½ orange

icing sugar, to taste

apple turnovers

Prepare the filling before rolling out the pastry. Mix together the chopped apple, lemon rind and ground cloves, if using, but do not add the sugar until the last minute because this will cause the juice to seep out of the apples. For the orange sugar, mix together the sugar and orange rind.

Preheat the oven to 220°C/425°F/Gas Mark 7. Roll the pastry out on a floured surface into a rectangle measuring 60 x 30 cm/ 24 x 12 inches. Cut the pastry in half lengthways, then across into four to make eight 15-cm/6-inch squares. (You can do this in two batches, rolling half of the pastry out into a 30-cm/ 12-inch square and cutting it into quarters, if preferred.)

Mix the sugar into the apple filling. Brush each square lightly with milk and place a little of the apple filling in the centre. Fold one corner over diagonally to meet the opposite one, making a triangular turnover, and press the edges together very firmly. Place on a non-stick baking sheet. Repeat with the remaining squares.

Brush the turnovers with milk and sprinkle with a little of the orange sugar. Bake for 15–20 minutes, until puffed and well browned. Cool the turnovers on a wire rack.

For the orange cream, whip the cream, and the orange rind and juice together until thick. Add a little sugar to taste and whip again until the cream just holds soft peaks. Serve the warm turnovers with dollops of orange cream.

makes 12

2 tbsp butter, cut into
small pieces, plus extra
for greasing

225 g/8 oz white bread flour

1/2 tsp salt

7 g/1/4 oz easy-blend
dried yeast

1 egg, beaten lightly

125 ml/4 fl oz tepid milk

2 tbsp maple syrup,
for glazing

for the filling

4 tbsp butter, softened

2 tsp ground cinnamon

50 g/13/4 oz soft light
brown sugar

50 g/13/4 oz currants

cinnamon swirls

Grease a baking sheet with a little butter.

Sift the flour and salt into a mixing bowl. Stir in the yeast. Rub
in the butter with your fingertips until the mixture resembles
breadcrumbs. Add the egg and milk and mix to form a dough.

Form the dough into a ball, place in a greased bowl, cover and
leave to stand in a warm place for about 40 minutes, or until
doubled in size.

Punch down the dough lightly for 1 minute, then roll out to a
rectangle measuring 30 x 23 cm/12 x 9 inches.

To make the filling, cream together the softened butter,
cinnamon and brown sugar until light and fluffy. Spread the
filling evenly over the dough rectangle, leaving a 2.5-cm/1-inch
border all around. Sprinkle the currants evenly over the top.

Roll up the dough from one of the long edges, and press down to
seal. Cut the roll into 12 slices. Place them, cut-side down, on the
baking sheet, cover and leave to stand for 30 minutes.

Preheat the oven to 190°C/375°F/Gas Mark 5. Bake the buns for
20–30 minutes, or until well risen. Brush with the maple syrup
and leave to cool slightly before serving.

makes 24

600 g/1 lb 5 oz white bread flour, plus extra for dusting

7 g/¼ oz easy-blend dried yeast

115 g/4 oz caster sugar

½ tsp salt

1 tsp ground cinnamon

85 g/3 oz unsalted butter

2 large eggs, plus 1 egg, beaten, for glazing

300 ml/10 fl oz milk

oil, for greasing

for the filling

6 tbsp chocolate hazelnut spread

200 g/7 oz milk chocolate, chopped

double-chocolate swirls

Mix together the flour, yeast, sugar, salt and cinnamon in a large bowl.

Melt the butter in a heatproof bowl set over a saucepan of gently simmering water, then allow to cool slightly. Whisk in the 2 eggs and milk. Pour into the flour mixture and mix well to form a dough.

Turn out onto a floured work surface and knead for 10 minutes until smooth. Put into a large floured bowl, cover with clingfilm and put in a warm place for 8 hours, or overnight.

When you are ready to make the buns, take the dough from the bowl and punch down. Preheat the oven to 220°C/425°F/Gas Mark 7 and lightly oil 2 baking sheets.

Divide the dough into 4 pieces and roll each piece into a rectangle about 2.5-cm/1-inch thick. Spread each rectangle with the chocolate hazelnut spread and scatter with the chopped chocolate. Roll up each piece from one of the long edges, then cut into 6 pieces. Place each swirl, cut-side down, on the baking sheets and brush each one well with the beaten egg. Bake in the preheated oven for 20 minutes and serve warm.

serves 6

2 tbsp butter, cut into
small pieces, plus extra
for greasing

225 g/8 oz white bread flour

1/2 tsp salt

7 g/1/4 oz easy-blend
dried yeast

125 ml/4 fl oz tepid milk

1 egg, beaten lightly

for the filling

4 tbsp butter, softened

50 g/13/4 oz soft light
brown sugar

2 tbsp chopped hazelnuts

1 tbsp chopped stem ginger

50 g/13/4 oz mixed
candied peel

1 tbsp dark rum or brandy

for the icing

115 g/4 oz icing sugar

2 tbsp lemon juice

crown loaf

Grease a baking sheet. Sift the flour and salt into a bowl. Stir in the yeast. Rub in the butter with your fingertips. Add the milk and egg and mix to form a dough.

Place the dough in a greased bowl, cover and stand in a warm place for 40 minutes, until doubled in size. Punch down the dough lightly for 1 minute. Roll out to a rectangle measuring about 30 x 23 cm/12 x 9 inches.

To make the filling, cream together the butter and sugar until light and fluffy. Stir in the hazelnuts, ginger, candied peel and rum or brandy. Spread the filling over the dough, leaving a 2.5-cm/1-inch border.

Roll up the dough, starting from one of the long edges, into a sausage shape. Cut into slices at 5-cm/2-inch intervals and place, cut-side down, in a circle on the baking sheet with the slices just touching. Cover and stand in a warm place to prove for 30 minutes.

Preheat the oven to 190°C/375°F/Gas Mark 5. Bake the loaf for 20–30 minutes, or until golden. Meanwhile, mix the icing sugar with enough lemon juice to form a thin icing.

Leave the loaf to cool slightly before drizzling with icing. Leave the icing to set slightly before serving.

makes 12

175 g/6 oz butter, softened, plus extra for greasing

500 g/1 lb 2 oz white bread flour

1/2 tsp salt

7 g/1/4 oz easy-blend dried yeast

2 tbsp lard or white vegetable fat

1 egg, beaten lightly

225 ml/8 fl oz tepid water

100 g/31/2 oz plain chocolate, broken into 12 squares

beaten egg, for glazing

pain au chocolat

Lightly grease a baking sheet. Sift the flour and salt into a mixing bowl and stir in the yeast. Rub in the lard or white vegetable fat with your fingertips. Add the egg and enough of the water to mix to a soft dough. Knead for about 10 minutes to make a smooth elastic dough.

Roll out to a 38 x 20-cm/15 x 8-inch rectangle and mark it vertically into thirds. Divide the butter into 3 portions and dot one portion over the first two-thirds of the rectangle, leaving a small border around the edge.

Fold the rectangle into 3 by first folding the plain part of the dough over and then the other side. Seal the edges of the dough by pressing with a rolling pin. Give the dough a quarter-turn so the sealed edges are at the top and bottom. Roll out the dough as big as the original rectangle and fold (without adding butter), then wrap the dough and chill for 30 minutes.

Repeat this rolling, folding and turning twice more until all of the butter has been used, chilling the dough each time. Re-roll and fold twice more without butter. Chill for a final 30 minutes.

Roll the dough out to 45 x 30 cm/18 x 12 inches, trim and halve lengthways. Cut each half into 6 rectangles and brush with beaten egg. Place a chocolate square at one end of each rectangle and roll up to form a sausage. Press the ends together and place, seam-side down, on the baking sheet. Cover and leave to prove for 40 minutes in a warm place. Preheat the oven to 220°C/425°F/Gas Mark 7. Brush each pastry roll with egg and bake in the oven for 20–25 minutes, until golden. Cool on a wire rack. Serve warm or cold.

serves 6

for the puff pastry

175 g/6 oz plain flour

pinch of salt

175 g/6 oz unsalted butter

about 150 ml/5 fl oz
chilled water

(or use 250 g/9 oz
ready-made puff pastry)

for the filling

6–8 just-ripe peaches

75 g/3 oz golden caster sugar

50 g/1¾ oz unsalted butter

3 pieces stem ginger in
syrup, chopped

1 tbsp ginger syrup from
the stem ginger jar

1 egg, beaten, for glazing

peach & ginger tarte tatin

To make the puff pastry, sift the flour and salt into a bowl and rub in 25 g/1 oz of the butter. Gradually add just enough water to bring the pastry together, and knead briefly to form a smooth dough. Wrap in clingfilm and chill for 30 minutes. Wrap the remaining butter in clingfilm and shape it into a 3-cm/1¼-inch thick rectangle. Roll out the dough to a rectangle 3 times longer and 3 cm/1¼ inches wider than the butter and place the butter in the centre, long-side towards you. Fold over the 2 'wings' of pastry to enclose the butter, press down the edges to seal and then turn the pastry so the short side faces you. Roll the pastry to its original length, fold into 3, turn and roll again to its original length. Repeat this once more then rewrap the pastry and chill again for 30 minutes. Remove from the refrigerator and repeat the rolling and turning twice more then chill again for 30 minutes.

Preheat the oven to 190°C/375°F/Gas Mark 5. Plunge the peaches into boiling water then drain and peel. Cut each in half. Put the sugar in a 25-cm/10-inch heavy, ovenproof frying pan and heat it gently until it caramelizes. Don't stir, just shake the pan if necessary. Once the sugar turns a dark caramel colour, remove from the heat and drop 25 g/1 oz of the butter into it.

Place the peaches cut-side up on top of the caramel, packing them as close together as possible and tucking the stem ginger pieces into any gaps. Dot with the remaining butter and drizzle with the ginger syrup. Return to a gentle heat while you roll out the pastry in a circle larger than the pan you are using. Drape the pastry over the peaches and tuck it in well around the edges, brush with the beaten egg and bake for 20–25 minutes, until the pastry is browned and puffed up. Remove from the oven and leave to rest for 5 minutes then invert onto a plate and serve.

makes 6

for the puff pastry

175 g/6 oz plain flour

pinch of salt

175 g/6 oz unsalted butter

about 150 ml/5 fl oz
chilled water

(or use 250 g/9 oz
ready-made puff pastry)

for the filling

1 large or 2 small aubergines,
trimmed and thinly sliced

5 tbsp olive oil

3 buffalo mozzarella
cheeses, sliced

6 tbsp pesto

black pepper

1 egg yolk, beaten, for glazing

6 slices Parma ham

aubergine, pesto &
parma ham tartlets

Prepare the puff pastry following the instructions on page 25.

When you are ready to make the tarts, cut the pastry into 6 and roll into either circles or rectangles then place on 2 baking trays, 3 on each. Preheat the oven to 190°C/375°F/Gas Mark 5.

Brush the aubergine slices with 2 tbsp of the olive oil and fry briefly in a non-stick frying pan, in batches, then arrange the slices neatly overlapping on each pastry base, leaving a 2.5-cm/ 1-inch margin around the edges. Lay the mozzarella slices over the aubergine slices and spoon over the pesto. Drizzle with the remaining olive oil and season with black pepper. Brush the edges of the pastry with egg yolk and bake for 15 minutes. Remove from the oven and drape a slice of Parma ham on each tart before serving.

serves 6

for the puff pastry

175 g/6 oz plain flour

pinch of salt

175 g/6 oz unsalted butter

about 150 ml/5 fl oz
chilled water

(or use 250 g/9 oz
ready-made puff pastry)

for the topping

500 g/1 lb 2 oz goat cheese,
such as chèvre, sliced

3–4 sprigs fresh thyme,
leaves picked from stalks

55 g/2 oz black olives,
pitted

50 g/1¾ oz tin anchovies in
olive oil

1 tbsp olive oil

salt and pepper

1 egg yolk, beaten, for glazing

goat's cheese & thyme tart

Prepare the puff pastry following the instructions on page 25.

Roll the pastry into a large circle or rectangle and place on a baking tray. Preheat the oven to 190°C/375°F/Gas Mark 5.

Arrange the cheese slices on the pastry, leaving a 2.5-cm/1-inch margin around the edge. Sprinkle the thyme and olives over the cheese and arrange the anchovies on top. Drizzle over the olive oil. Season well and brush the edges of the pastry with the egg. Bake for 20–25 minutes, until the cheese is bubbling and the pastry is browned.

So Choux

makes 12

for the choux pastry

70 g/2½ oz butter, cut
into small pieces, plus
extra for greasing

150 ml/5 fl oz water

100 g/3½ oz plain flour,
sifted

2 eggs

for the pastry cream

2 eggs, beaten lightly

4 tbsp caster sugar

2 tbsp cornflour

300 ml/10 fl oz milk

¼ tsp vanilla essence

for the icing

2 tbsp butter

1 tbsp milk

1 tbsp cocoa powder

55 g/2 oz icing sugar

white chocolate, broken into
pieces

chocolate éclairs

Preheat the oven to 200°C/400°F/Gas Mark 6. Lightly grease a
baking sheet. Place the water in a saucepan, add the butter
and heat gently until the butter melts. Bring to a rolling boil,
then remove the saucepan from the heat and add the flour all
at once, beating well until the mixture leaves the sides of the
saucepan and forms a ball. Leave to cool slightly, then gradually
beat in the eggs to form a smooth, glossy mixture. Spoon into a
large piping bag fitted with a 1-cm/½-inch plain nozzle.

Sprinkle the baking sheet with a little water. Pipe éclairs 7.5 cm/
3 inches long, spaced well apart. Bake in the preheated oven for
30–35 minutes, or until crisp and golden. Make a small slit in
the side of each éclair to let the steam escape. Leave to cool on a
wire rack.

Meanwhile, make the pastry cream. Whisk the eggs and sugar
until thick and creamy, then fold in the cornflour. Heat the milk
until almost boiling and pour onto the eggs, whisking. Transfer
to the saucepan and cook over a low heat, stirring until thick.
Remove the saucepan from the heat and stir in the vanilla
essence. Cover with baking paper and leave to cool.

To make the icing, melt the butter with the milk in a saucepan,
remove from the heat and stir in the cocoa and sugar. Split the
éclairs lengthways and pipe in the pastry cream. Spread the
icing over the top of the éclairs. Melt a little white chocolate in a
heatproof bowl set over a saucepan of gently simmering water,
then drizzle over the chocolate icing and leave to set.

makes 12
for the choux pastry
55 g/2 oz butter
150 ml/5 fl oz water
70 g/2½ oz plain flour, sifted
2 eggs, beaten

for the filling and topping
175 ml/6 fl oz double cream
1 tbsp icing sugar
175 g/6 oz fresh raspberries
85 g/3 oz plain chocolate,
broken into pieces

raspberry chocolate éclairs

Preheat the oven to 220°C/425°F/Gas Mark 7. To make the choux pastry, place the butter and water in a heavy-based saucepan and bring to the boil over a low heat. Add the flour, all at once, and beat thoroughly until the mixture leaves the side of the saucepan. Leave to cool slightly, then vigorously beat in the eggs, a little at a time.

Spoon the mixture into a piping bag fitted with a 1-cm/½-inch nozzle and pipe 7.5-cm/3-inch lengths onto a dampened baking sheet. Bake in the preheated oven for 10 minutes, then reduce the oven temperature to 190°C/375°F/Gas Mark 5 and bake for an additional 20 minutes, or until crisp and golden brown. Split the side of each éclair to let the steam escape, and transfer to a wire rack to cool completely.

To make the filling, place the cream and icing sugar in a bowl and whip until thick. Split the éclairs lengthways and spoon in the cream mixture. Place a few raspberries in each éclair.

Melt the chocolate in a heatproof bowl set over a saucepan of gently simmering water. Spread a little on top of each éclair. Leave to set, then serve.

coffee caramel éclairs

makes 12

for the choux pastry

150 ml/5 fl oz water

55 g/2 oz butter, plus extra
for greasing

70 g/2¹/₂ oz plain flour, sifted

2 eggs, lightly beaten

for the filling

300 ml/10 fl oz double cream

4 tbsp rum

1 tbsp icing sugar

for the coffee caramel

200 g/7 oz sugar

8 tbsp water

1 tsp instant coffee

Place the water and butter in a saucepan and heat gently until the butter melts, then turn up the heat and bring it rapidly to the boil. Immediately add all the flour, remove the pan from the heat and stir the mixture into a paste that leaves the sides of the pan clean. Do not beat or it will become greasy. Allow to cool slightly for about 15 minutes.

Meanwhile, preheat the oven to 220°C/425°F/Gas Mark 7. Grease a baking sheet and prepare a piping bag fitted with a plain 1.5-cm/ ³/₄-inch tube. Gradually beat the eggs into the flour paste and continue beating until it is smooth and glossy. Spoon the paste into the bag and pipe 12 strips of paste on the baking sheet.

Bake for 15 minutes. Reduce the oven temperature to 190°C/375°F/ Gas Mark 5 and cook for a further 20–25 minutes, until the éclairs are risen, well browned and crisp. Transfer to a wire rack, slitting each pastry lengthways to allow the steam to escape. Leave to cool.

For the filling, whip the cream with the rum and icing sugar. Pipe this into the pastries and return them to the wire rack placing it over a baking sheet. Keep the pastries close together.

For the caramel, place the sugar in a pan and add the water. Heat gently, stirring occasionally, until the sugar has dissolved. Then bring to the boil and boil rapidly, without stirring, until the syrup turns golden. Remove from the heat and stir in the coffee using a metal fork. Immediately drizzle the coffee caramel over the éclairs. Leave to set and cool, then use kitchen scissors to snip any drizzles of set caramel between the éclairs.

makes 12

for the choux pastry

150 ml/5 fl oz water

55 g/2 oz butter, plus extra
for greasing

70 g/2¹/2 oz plain flour, sifted

2 eggs, lightly beaten

for the filling and topping

4 passion fruit

350 g/12 oz mascarpone
cheese

400 g/14 oz white chocolate

crystallized rose petals or
violets, to decorate (optional)

white chocolate passion éclairs

Place the water and butter in a saucepan and heat gently until the butter melts, then turn up the heat and bring it rapidly to the boil. Immediately add all the flour, remove the pan from the heat and stir the mixture into a paste that leaves the sides of the pan clean. Do not beat or it will become greasy. Allow to cool slightly for about 15 minutes.

Meanwhile, preheat the oven to 220°C/425°F/Gas Mark 7. Grease a baking sheet and prepare a piping bag fitted with a plain 1.5-cm/ ¾-inch tube. Gradually beat the eggs into the flour paste and continue beating until it is smooth and glossy. Spoon the paste into the bag and pipe 12 strips of paste on the baking sheet.

Bake for 15 minutes. Reduce the oven temperature to 190°C/ 375°F/Gas Mark 5 and cook for a further 20–25 minutes, until the éclairs are risen, well browned and crisp. Transfer to a wire rack, slitting each pastry lengthways to allow the steam to escape. Leave to cool.

Halve the passion fruit and scoop out the flesh into a sieve over a bowl. Press out all the juice and discard the seeds. Mix the juice into the mascarpone.

Melt 175 g/6 oz of the chocolate in a heatproof bowl over a pan of gently simmering water, stirring occasionally. Stir this into the mascarpone. Melt the remaining chocolate.

Fill the éclairs with the mascarpone mixture. Coat the tops with the melted white chocolate. Add a little piece of crystallized rose petal or violet on top of each, if liked, and leave to set before serving.

makes 12

for the filling and topping

2 tsp powdered gelatine

2 tbsp water

350 g/12 oz strawberries

225 g/8 oz ricotta cheese

1 tbsp caster sugar

2 tsp crème de fraises de bois

icing sugar, for dusting

for the petits choux

100 g/3$\frac{1}{2}$ oz plain flour

2 tbsp cocoa powder

pinch of salt

6 tbsp unsalted butter

225 ml/8 fl oz water

2 eggs, plus 1 egg white, beaten

strawberry petits choux

Sprinkle the gelatine over the water in a heatproof bowl. Let it soften for 2 minutes. Place the bowl over a saucepan of simmering water and stir until the gelatine dissolves. Remove from the heat.

Place 225 g/8 oz of the strawberries in a blender with the ricotta, sugar and liqueur. Process until blended. Add the gelatine and process briefly. Transfer the mousse to a bowl, cover with clingfilm and chill for 1–1½ hours, until set.

Meanwhile, make the petits choux. Line a baking tray with baking parchment. Sift together the flour, cocoa powder and salt. Put the butter and water into a heavy-based saucepan and heat gently until the butter has melted.

Preheat the oven to 220°C/425°F/Gas Mark 7. Remove the saucepan from the heat and add the flour, cocoa powder and salt all at once, stirring well until the mixture leaves the sides of the saucepan. Leave to cool slightly.

Gradually beat the eggs into the flour paste and continue beating until it is smooth and glossy. Drop 12 rounded tablespoonfuls of the mixture onto the prepared baking sheet and bake for 20–25 minutes, until puffed up and crisp.

Remove from the oven and make a slit in the side of each petit chou. Return to the oven for 5 minutes. Transfer to a wire rack.

Slice the remaining strawberries. Cut the petits choux in half, divide the mousse and strawberry slices among them, then replace the tops. Dust lightly with icing sugar and place in the refrigerator. Serve within 1½ hours.

serves 4

for the choux pastry

5 tbsp butter, plus extra
for greasing

200 ml/7 fl oz water

100 g/3$^1/_2$ oz plain flour

3 eggs, beaten

for the cream filling

300 ml/10 fl oz double cream

3 tbsp caster sugar

1 tsp vanilla essence

for the chocolate sauce

125 g/4$^1/_2$ oz dark chocolate,
broken into small pieces

2$^1/_2$ tbsp butter

6 tbsp water

2 tbsp brandy

profiteroles with chocolate sauce

Preheat the oven to 200°C/400°F/Gas Mark 6. Grease a large baking sheet with butter. To make the pastry, put the water and butter into a saucepan and bring to the boil. Meanwhile, sift the flour into a bowl. Immediately add all the flour, remove the pan from the heat and stir the mixture into a paste that leaves the sides of the saucepan clean. Leave to cool slightly. Beat in enough of the eggs to give the mixture a soft, dropping consistency.

Transfer to a piping bag fitted with a 1-cm/½-inch plain nozzle. Pipe small balls onto the baking sheet. Bake for 25 minutes. Remove from the oven. Pierce each ball with a skewer to let the steam escape.

To make the filling, whip together the cream, sugar and vanilla essence. Cut the pastry balls almost in half, then fill with cream.

To make the sauce, gently melt the chocolate and butter with the water in a heatproof bowl set over a saucepan of gently simmering water, stirring, until smooth. Stir in the brandy. Pile the profiteroles into individual serving dishes or into a pyramid on a raised cake stand. Pour over the sauce and serve.

makes 4

for the choux pastry

150 ml/5 fl oz water

55 g/2 oz butter, plus extra
for greasing

70 g/2$\frac{1}{2}$ oz plain flour, sifted

2 eggs, lightly beaten

25 g/1 oz flaked almonds

for the filling

grated rind of 2 lemons

2 tbsp icing sugar,
plus extra for dusting

350 g/12 oz low-fat soft
cheese, such as quark
or curd cheese

juice of $\frac{1}{2}$ lemon

blueberries, raspberries or
strawberries, to serve
(optional)

lemon cheesecake rings

Place the water and butter in a saucepan and heat gently until the butter melts, then turn up the heat and bring it rapidly to the boil. Immediately add all the flour, remove the pan from the heat and stir the mixture into a paste that leaves the sides of the pan clean. Do not beat or it will become greasy. Allow to cool slightly for about 15 minutes.

Preheat the oven to 220°C/425°F/Gas Mark 7. Grease a baking sheet. Gradually beat the eggs into the flour paste and continue beating until the mixture is smooth and glossy. Spoon dollops of the paste onto the baking sheet, shaping it into 4 rings of about 10 cm/4 inches in diameter, making sure that they are well spaced. Sprinkle with flaked almonds and press them gently onto the paste with the point of a knife.

Bake for 15 minutes. Reduce the oven temperature to 180°C/350°F/Gas Mark 4 and cook for a further 20–25 minutes, until the rings are risen, well browned and crisp. Transfer to a wire rack, and use a serrated knife to slice each ring horizontally in half. Leave to cool.

For the filling, place the lemon rind, icing sugar and soft cheese in a bowl and mix well, adding lemon juice to taste. Chill until ready to serve the rings. Spoon or pipe the filling on the bottom layers of the rings and replace the tops. Sift over a little icing sugar and serve with the soft fruit, if liked.

makes 20

for the choux fritters

540 g/1 lb 4 oz can pineapple pieces in natural juice

55 g/2 oz butter

70 g/2$^{1}/_{2}$ oz plain flour, sifted

2 eggs, lightly beaten

grated rind of 1 orange

oil, for deep-frying

for the ginger-wine honey

1 tsp arrowroot or cornflour

4 tbsp ginger wine

3 tbsp clear honey

2 pieces preserved ginger, cut into slivers

pineapple choux fritters

Drain the pineapple, reserving the juice. Check through the pineapple pieces, snipping any large ones in half with scissors, and set aside. Measure 150 ml/5 fl oz of the pineapple juice into a pan. Add the butter and heat gently until the butter melts, then turn up the heat and bring rapidly to the boil. Immediately add all the flour, remove the pan from the heat and stir the mixture into a paste that leaves the sides of the pan clean. Do not beat or it will become greasy. Allow to cool slightly for about 15 minutes.

Meanwhile, for the ginger-wine honey, mix the arrowroot or cornflour to a paste with the ginger wine in a small pan, then stir in the honey. Bring to the boil, stirring continuously, and remove from the heat. Stir in the preserved ginger. Set aside.

Heat the oil for deep-frying to 190°C/375°F or until a cube of bread browns in about 1 minute. Beat the eggs into the flour paste, then beat in the orange rind until the paste is glossy. Stir in the pineapple until just mixed.

Deep-fry spoonfuls of the pineapple mixture turning once or twice, for 3–5 minutes, until puffed and golden. Drain on kitchen paper and keep warm until all the fritters are cooked. Pile the choux fritters into dishes. Stir the ginger-wine honey and drizzle it over the fritters. Serve at once.

makes 22

for the choux pastry

55 g/2 oz butter, plus extra for greasing

150 ml/5 fl oz water

70 g/2½ oz plain flour, sifted

2 eggs, beaten

for the filling

2 tbsp mayonnaise

1 tsp tomato purée

140 g/5 oz small prawns, cooked and peeled

1 tsp Worcestershire sauce

salt

Tabasco sauce

1 Little Gem lettuce, shredded

cayenne pepper, to garnish

mini choux puffs with prawn cocktail

Preheat the oven to 180°C/350°F/Gas Mark 4, then grease a baking sheet. To make the choux pastry, place the butter and water in a large, heavy-based saucepan and bring to the boil. Immediately add all the flour, remove the pan from the heat and stir the mixture into a paste that leaves the sides of the saucepan clean. Leave to cool slightly, then vigorously beat in the eggs, one at a time. Place 22 walnut-sized spoonfuls of the mixture onto the baking sheet, spaced 2 cm/¾ inch apart. Bake in the preheated oven for 35 minutes, or until light, crisp and golden. Transfer to a wire rack to cool, then cut a 5-mm/¼-inch slice from the top of each puff.

To make the filling, place the mayonnaise, tomato purée, prawns and Worcestershire sauce in a bowl. Add salt and Tabasco sauce to taste, and mix together until combined.

Place a few lettuce shreds in the bottom of each puff, making sure some protrude at the top. Spoon the prawn mixture on top and dust with a little cayenne pepper before serving.

makes 24

150 ml/5 fl oz water

55 g/2 oz butter, plus extra
for greasing

70 g/2¹/₂ oz plain flour, sifted

2 eggs, lightly beaten

4 tbsp finely chopped
spring onions

grated rind of 1 lemon

1 garlic clove, crushed

50 g/2 oz blue cheese, such as
Danish blue, finely crumbled

75 g/3 oz pitted black olives
(about 24)

blue cheese & olive gougères

Place the water and butter in a saucepan and heat gently until
the butter melts, then turn up the heat and bring it rapidly to
the boil. Immediately add all the flour, remove the pan from the
heat and stir the mixture into a paste that leaves the sides of
the pan clean. Do not beat or it will become greasy. Allow to cool
slightly for about 15 minutes.

Meanwhile, preheat the oven to 220°C/425°F/Gas Mark 7. Grease
two baking sheets. Gradually beat the eggs into the flour paste,
then beat in the spring onions, lemon rind and garlic until the
paste is smooth and glossy. Beat in the blue cheese.

Use two teaspoons to spoon small mounds of the mixture on the
baking sheets (or pipe it from a bag with a plain nozzle). Press
an olive into each mound. Bake for about 20 minutes, until well
risen, crisp and browned. Transfer to a wire rack and cool briefly
before serving hot, warm or cold.

Fancy Filo

makes 4

1 eating apple

1 ripe pear

2 tbsp lemon juice

55 g/2 oz low-fat spread

4 sheets filo pastry,
thawed if frozen

2 tbsp apricot jam

1 tbsp orange juice

1 tbsp chopped pistachio nuts

2 tsp icing sugar, for dusting

paper-thin fruit pies

Preheat the oven to 200°C/400°F/Gas Mark 6. Core and thinly slice the apple and pear and immediately toss them in the lemon juice to prevent them from turning brown. Melt the low-fat spread in a saucepan over a low heat.

Cut each sheet of pastry into 4 and cover with a clean, damp tea towel. Brush a 4-cup non-stick muffin tin (cup size 10 cm/ 4 inches in diameter) with a little of the low-fat spread.

Working on each pie separately, brush 4 small sheets of pastry with low-fat spread. Press a sheet of pastry into the base of 1 cup. Arrange the other sheets of pastry on top at slightly different angles. Repeat with the other sheets of pastry to make another 3 pies.

Arrange the apple and pear slices alternately in the centre of each pie case and lightly crimp the edge of the pastry of each pie.

Stir the jam and orange juice together until smooth and brush over the fruit. Bake in the preheated oven for 12–15 minutes. Sprinkle with the pistachio nuts, dust lightly with icing sugar and serve hot straight from the oven.

makes 25

225 g/8 oz walnut halves

225 g/8 oz shelled
pistachio nuts

100 g/3$\frac{1}{2}$ oz blanched
almonds

4 tbsp pine kernels,
finely chopped

finely grated rind of
2 large oranges

6 tbsp sesame seeds

1 tbsp sugar

$\frac{1}{2}$ tsp ground cinnamon

$\frac{1}{2}$ tsp mixed spice

250 g/9 oz butter, melted,
plus extra for greasing

23 sheets filo pastry,
thawed if frozen

for the syrup

450 g/1 lb caster sugar

450 ml/16 fl oz water

5 tbsp honey

3 cloves

2 large strips lemon zest

baklava

To make the filling, put the walnuts, pistachio nuts, almonds and pine kernels in a food processor and process gently, until finely chopped but not ground. Transfer the chopped nuts to a bowl and stir in the orange rind, sesame seeds, sugar, cinnamon and mixed spice.

Grease a 25-cm/10-inch square (or similar) ovenproof dish that is 5 cm/2 inches deep. Preheat the oven to 160°C/325°F/Gas Mark 3. Cut the stacked filo sheets to size, using a ruler. Keep the sheets covered with a damp cloth. Place a sheet of filo on the bottom of the dish and brush with melted butter. Top with 7 more sheets, brushing with butter between each layer.

Sprinkle with a generous 150 g/5 oz of the nutty filling. Top with 3 sheets of filo, brushing each one with butter. Continue layering until you have used up all the filo and filling, ending with a top layer of 3 filo sheets. Brush with butter.

Using a sharp knife cut the baklava into 5-cm/2-inch squares. Brush again with butter. Bake in the preheated oven for 1 hour.

Meanwhile, put all the syrup ingredients in a saucepan. Slowly bring to the boil, stirring to dissolve the sugar, then simmer for 15 minutes, without stirring, until a thin syrup forms. Leave to cool.

Remove the baklava from the oven and pour the syrup over the top. Leave to cool in the dish, then cut out the squares to serve.

makes 18

55 g/2 oz plain chocolate, broken into pieces

85 g/3 oz ground hazelnuts

1 tbsp finely chopped fresh mint

125 ml/4 fl oz soured cream

2 eating apples

9 sheets filo pastry, about 15 cm/6 inches square, thawed if frozen

55–85 g/2–3 oz butter, melted

icing sugar, for dusting

chocolate filo parcels

Preheat the oven to 190°C/375°F/Gas Mark 5. Melt the chocolate in a heatproof bowl set over a saucepan of gently simmering water. Remove from the heat and leave to cool slightly.

Mix together the hazelnuts, mint and soured cream in a bowl. Peel the apples and grate them into the bowl, then stir in the melted chocolate and mix well.

Cut each sheet of filo pastry into 4 squares. Keep the squares you are not using covered with a damp cloth. Brush 1 square with melted butter, place a second square on top and brush with melted butter. Place a tablespoonful of the chocolate mixture in the centre, then bring up the corners of the squares and twist together to enclose the filling completely. Continue making parcels in the same way until you have used up all the pastry and filling.

Brush a baking sheet with melted butter and place the parcels on it. Bake for about 10 minutes until crisp and golden. Leave to cool slightly, then dust with icing sugar.

makes 20

4 tbsp butter, melted,
plus extra for greasing

10 sheets filo pastry,
thawed if frozen

for the filling

75 g/2¾ oz pistachio nuts,
ground coarsely

50 g/1¾ oz ground hazelnuts

2 tbsp golden granulated
sugar

1 tbsp rosewater

55 g/2 oz plain chocolate,
grated

icing sugar, for dusting

pistachio pastries

Preheat the oven to 180°C/350°F/Gas Mark 4. Grease 2 baking sheets. To make the filling, put the pistachio nuts and hazelnuts in a bowl with the sugar, rosewater and chocolate. Mix together. Cut each sheet of filo pastry lengthways in half. Pile the rectangles on top of each other and cover with a damp tea towel to prevent them drying out.

Brush a filo sheet with melted butter. Spread a teaspoon of filling along one short end. Fold the long sides in, slightly over the filling and roll up from the filling end. Place on the prepared baking sheets with the seam underneath and brush with melted butter.

Repeat with the remaining pastry and filling. Bake in the preheated oven for 20 minutes, or until crisp and very lightly coloured. Transfer to a wire rack to cool. Dust with icing sugar before serving.

serves 2–4

8 crisp eating apples

1 tbsp lemon juice

115 g/4 oz sultanas

1 tsp ground cinnamon

1/2 tsp grated nutmeg

1 tbsp soft light brown sugar

6 sheets filo pastry,
thawed if frozen

vegetable oil spray

icing sugar, to serve

for the sauce

1 tbsp cornflour

450 ml/16 fl oz dry cider

apple strudel & cider sauce

Preheat the oven to 190°C/375°F/Gas Mark 5. Line a baking tray with baking paper.

Peel and core the apples and chop them into 1-cm/1/2-inch dice. Toss the apples in a bowl with the lemon juice, sultanas, cinnamon, nutmeg and brown sugar.

Lay out a sheet of filo pastry, spray with vegetable oil and lay a second sheet on top. Repeat with a third sheet. Spread over half the apple mixture and roll up lengthways, tucking in the ends to enclose the filling. Repeat to make a second strudel. Slide onto the baking tray, spray with oil and bake for 15–20 minutes.

To make the sauce, blend the cornflour in a saucepan with a little dry cider until smooth. Add the remaining cider and heat gently, stirring, until the mixture boils and thickens. Serve the strudel warm or cold, dredged with icing sugar, and accompanied by the cider sauce.

serves 4

2 ripe pears

55 g/2 oz butter

55 g/2 oz fresh white breadcrumbs

55 g/2 oz shelled pecan nuts, chopped

25 g/1 oz light muscovado sugar

finely grated rind of 1 orange

100 g/3 1/2 oz filo pastry, thawed if frozen

6 tbsp orange blossom honey

2 tbsp orange juice

icing sugar, for dusting

Greek-style yogurt, to serve (optional)

pear & pecan strudel

Preheat the oven to 200°C/400°F/Gas Mark 6. Peel, core and chop the pears. Melt 1 tablespoon of the butter in a frying pan and gently fry the breadcrumbs until golden. Transfer to a bowl and add the pears, nuts, muscovado sugar and orange rind. Put the remaining butter in a small saucepan and heat until melted.

Reserve 1 sheet of filo pastry, keeping it well wrapped, and brush the remaining filo sheets with a little melted butter. Spoon a little of the nut filling onto the first filo sheet, leaving a 2.5-cm/ 1-inch margin around the edge. Build up the strudel by placing buttered filo sheets on top of the first, spreading each one with nut filling as you build up the layers. Drizzle the honey and orange juice over the top.

Fold the short ends over the filling, then roll up, starting at a long side. Carefully lift onto a baking sheet, with the seam on top. Brush with any remaining melted butter and crumple the reserved sheet of filo pastry around the strudel. Bake for 25 minutes, or until golden and crisp. Dust with icing sugar and serve warm with Greek-style yogurt, if using.

serves 6

150 g/5¹/2 oz butter,
preferably unsalted,
plus extra for greasing

200 g/7 oz mixed chopped
nuts

115 g/4 oz plain chocolate,
chopped

115 g/4 oz milk chocolate,
chopped

115 g/4 oz white chocolate,
chopped

200 g/7 oz filo pastry,
thawed if frozen

3 tbsp golden syrup

55 g/2 oz icing sugar

chocolate nut strudel

Preheat the oven to 190°C/375°F/Gas Mark 5. Lightly grease a baking sheet with butter. Reserve 1 tablespoon of the nuts. Place the remaining nuts in a bowl and mix together with the 3 types of chocolate.

Place 1 sheet of filo pastry on a clean tea towel. Melt the butter and brush the sheet of filo with the butter, drizzle with a little syrup and sprinkle with some nuts and chocolate. Place another sheet of filo on top and repeat until you have used all the nuts and chocolate.

Use the tea towel to help you carefully roll up the strudel and place on the baking sheet, drizzle with a little more syrup and sprinkle with the reserved nuts. Bake in the preheated oven for 20–25 minutes. If the nuts start to brown too much, cover the strudel with a sheet of foil. Sprinkle the strudel with icing sugar, slice and serve.

makes 12

1 banana

25 g/1 oz chocolate chips

4 sheets filo pastry,
thawed if frozen

4 tbsp butter, melted

for the chocolate sauce

150 ml/5 fl oz single cream

55 g/2 oz plain chocolate,
broken into pieces

banana & chocolate triangles

Preheat the oven to 180°C/350°F/Gas Mark 4. Peel the banana, put in a bowl and mash with a fork. Stir in the chocolate chips. Cover the filo sheets with a damp tea towel to prevent them drying out. Brush a filo sheet with melted butter and cut lengthways into 3 strips, each about 6 cm/2½ inches wide.

Spoon a little of the banana mixture onto the bottom end of each strip, fold the corner of the pastry over to enclose it in a triangle and continue folding along the whole length of the strip to make a triangular parcel. Place on a baking sheet with the seam underneath. Repeat with the remaining pastry and filling. Bake in the preheated oven for 10–12 minutes, until golden.

To make the chocolate sauce, put the cream and chocolate in a heatproof bowl set over a saucepan of gently simmering water and stir until the chocolate has melted. Serve the pastries with the chocolate sauce.

makes 20

for the tartlet cases

70 g/2¹/₂ oz filo pastry, thawed if frozen

3 tbsp melted butter, plus extra for greasing

for the avocado salsa

1 large avocado

1 small red onion, finely chopped

1 fresh chilli, deseeded and finely chopped

2 tomatoes, peeled, deseeded and finely chopped

juice of 1 lime

2 tbsp chopped fresh coriander

salt and pepper

filo tartlets with avocado salsa

Preheat the oven to 180°C/350°F/Gas Mark 4. To make the tartlet cases, working with 1 sheet of filo pastry at a time and keeping the rest covered with a damp cloth, brush the pastry sheet with melted butter. With a sharp knife, cut the sheet into 5-cm/2-inch squares.

Grease 20 cups in mini muffin trays and line each one with 3 buttered filo pastry squares, setting each one at an angle to the others. Repeat until all the pastry is used up. Bake in the preheated oven for 6–8 minutes, or until crisp and golden. Carefully transfer to a wire rack to cool.

To make the salsa, peel the avocado and remove the stone. Cut the flesh into small dice and place in a bowl with the onion, chilli, tomatoes, lime juice and coriander, and add salt and pepper to taste. Divide the salsa between the pastry cases and serve immediately.

makes 12

85 g/3 oz butter, melted,
plus extra for greasing

200 g/7 oz fresh or canned
crabmeat, drained

6 spring onions, finely
chopped

2.5-cm/1-inch piece of
fresh root ginger, peeled
and grated

2 tsp soy sauce

pepper

12 sheets filo pastry,
thawed if frozen

crab & ginger triangles

Preheat the oven to 180°C/350°F/Gas Mark 4, then grease a baking sheet. Place the crabmeat, spring onions, ginger and soy sauce in a bowl, add pepper to taste, mix together and reserve. Working with 1 sheet of filo pastry at a time and keeping the rest covered with a damp cloth, brush a pastry sheet with melted butter, fold in half lengthways and brush again with butter.

Place a spoonful of the crab mixture in one corner of the pastry strip. Fold the pastry and filling over at right angles to make a triangle enclosing the filling. Continue folding in this way all the way down the strip to make a triangular parcel.

Place the parcel on the prepared baking sheet. Repeat with the remaining pastry and crab mixture. Brush each parcel with melted butter. Bake in the preheated oven for 20–25 minutes, or until crisp and golden brown. Serve warm.

4

Short & Simple

makes 6

for the pastry

175 g/6 oz plain flour

pinch of salt

55 g/2 oz butter, cut into small pieces

55 g/2 oz lard or white vegetable fat, cut into small pieces

2–3 tbsp cold water

for the filling

4 tbsp cornflour

400 ml/14 fl oz canned coconut milk

grated rind and juice of 2 limes

2 eggs, separated

175 g/6 oz caster sugar

lime & coconut meringue pies

To make the pastry, sift the flour and salt into a large bowl and rub in the butter and fat with the fingertips until the mixture resembles breadcrumbs. Add a little water and work the mixture together until a soft dough has formed. Wrap the dough and chill in the refrigerator for 30 minutes.

Preheat the oven to 180°C/350°F/Gas Mark 4. Roll out the pastry and use to line 6 pastry cases, each 10 cm/4 inches in diameter and 3 cm/1½ inches deep. Line with baking paper and fill with baking beans. Bake in the preheated oven for 15 minutes. Take the pastry cases out of the oven and remove the beans and paper. Reduce the oven temperature to 160°C/325°F/Gas Mark 3.

To make the filling, put the cornflour in a saucepan with a little of the coconut milk and stir to make a smooth paste. Stir in the rest of the coconut milk. Gradually bring to the boil over a low heat, stirring constantly. Cook, stirring, for 3 minutes until thickened. Remove from the heat and add the lime rind and juice, egg yolks and 4 tablespoons of the sugar. Pour the mixture into the pastry cases.

Put the egg whites in a clean, grease-free bowl and whisk until very stiff, then gradually whisk in the remaining sugar. Pipe the meringue into peaks over the filling to cover it completely, or cover the filling with the meringue and swirl gently with a palette knife. Bake the pies in the oven for 20 minutes, or until the tops are lightly browned. Serve hot or cold.

makes 12

for the pastry

200 g/7 oz plain flour,
plus extra for dusting

85 g/3 oz icing sugar

55 g/2 oz ground almonds

115 g/4 oz butter

1 egg yolk

1 tbsp milk

for the filling

225 g/8 oz cream cheese

icing sugar, to taste,
plus extra for dusting

350 g/12 oz fresh summer
fruits, such as red and
whitecurrants, blueberries,
raspberries and small
strawberries

summer fruit tartlets

To make the pastry, sift the flour and icing sugar into a bowl.
Stir in the ground almonds. Add the butter and rub in until the
mixture resembles breadcrumbs. Add the egg yolk and milk and
work in with a palette knife, then mix with your fingertips until
the dough binds together. Wrap the dough in clingfilm and leave
to chill in the refrigerator for 30 minutes.

Preheat the oven to 200°C/400°F/Gas Mark 6. Roll out the pastry
on a lightly floured work surface and use it to line 12 deep tartlet
or individual brioche tins. Prick the bases with a fork. Press a
piece of foil into each tartlet, covering the edges, and bake in the
preheated oven for 10–15 minutes, or until light golden brown.
Remove the foil and bake for a further 2–3 minutes. Transfer the
pastry cases to a wire rack to cool.

To make the filling, place the cream cheese and icing sugar in a
bowl and mix together. Place a spoonful of filling in each pastry
case and arrange the fruit on top. Dust with sifted icing sugar
and serve immediately.

makes 12

for the pastry

140 g/5 oz plain flour, plus extra for dusting

85 g/3 oz butter, cut into small pieces

55 g/2 oz golden caster sugar

2 egg yolks

for the filling

2 tbsp maple syrup

150 ml/5 fl oz double cream

115 g/4 oz golden caster sugar

pinch of cream of tartar

6 tbsp water

115 g/4 oz shelled pecan nuts, chopped

12–24 pecan nut halves, to decorate

maple pecan pies

To make the pastry, sift the flour into a mixing bowl and rub in the butter with your fingertips until the mixture resembles breadcrumbs. Add the sugar and egg yolks and mix to form a soft dough. Wrap the dough and chill in the refrigerator for 30 minutes. Preheat the oven to 200°C/400°F/Gas Mark 6.

On a lightly floured work surface, roll out the pastry thinly, cut out 12 circles and use to line 12 tartlet tins. Prick the bases with a fork. Line each tin with baking paper and fill with baking beans. Bake in the preheated oven for 10–15 minutes until light golden. Remove the paper and beans and bake for a further 2–3 minutes. Leave to cool on a wire rack.

Mix half the maple syrup and half the cream in a bowl. Put the sugar, cream of tartar and water in a saucepan and heat gently until the sugar dissolves. Bring to the boil and boil until light golden. Remove from the heat and stir in the maple syrup and cream mixture.

Return the saucepan to the heat and cook to the soft ball stage (116°C/240°F): that is, when a little of the mixture dropped into a bowl of cold water forms a soft ball. Stir in the remaining cream and leave until cool. Brush the remaining maple syrup over the edges of the pies. Put the chopped pecan nuts in the pastry cases and spoon in the toffee. Top each pie with 1 or 2 pecan halves. Leave to cool completely before serving.

florentine praline tartlets

makes 6

for the praline

100 g/3½ oz sugar

3 tbsp water

50 g/1¾ oz flaked almonds

butter, for greasing

for the pastry

125 g/4½ oz plain flour, plus extra for dusting

pinch of salt

75 g/2½ oz cold butter, cut into pieces

1 tsp icing sugar

cold water

for the frangipane

75 g/2½ oz butter

2 eggs

75 g/2½ oz caster sugar

25 g/1 oz plain flour

100 g/3½ oz ground almonds

for the topping

8 glacé cherries, chopped, plus extra to decorate

25 g/1 oz mixed candied peel, chopped

100 g/3½ oz plain chocolate, chopped

First make the praline. Put the sugar and the water in a saucepan and dissolve the sugar over a low heat. Do not stir the sugar, just let it boil for 10 minutes, until it turns to caramel, then stir in the flaked almonds and turn out onto buttered foil. Allow to cool and harden. When cold, break up the praline and chop into smallish pieces.

Butter 6 x 9-cm/3½-inch loose-bottomed fluted tart tins. Sift the flour and salt into a food processor, add the butter and process until the mixture resembles fine breadcrumbs. Tip the mixture into a large bowl, add the icing sugar and a little cold water, just enough to bring the dough together. Turn out onto a floured surface and divide into 6 equal-sized pieces. Roll each piece to fit the tart tins. Carefully fit each piece of pastry in its case and press well to fit the tin. Roll the rolling pin over the tin to neaten the edges and trim the excess pastry. Put in the freezer for 30 minutes. Meanwhile, preheat the oven to 200°C/400°F/Gas Mark 6.

While the tarts are in the freezer, make the frangipane. Melt the butter and beat the eggs and caster sugar together. Stir the melted butter into the egg and sugar mixture, then add the flour and ground almonds. Remove the tart tins from the freezer. Line with baking paper and dried beans and bake for 10 minutes. Remove the paper and beans, then divide the frangipane among the tart shells and return to the oven for 8–10 minutes.

While the tarts are baking, mix the cherries, peel, chocolate and praline together. Divide among the tarts while they are still hot so that some of the chocolate melts. Serve cold, decorated with glacé cherries.

makes 12

for the pastry

225 g/8 oz plain flour,
plus extra for dusting

2 tbsp golden caster sugar

150 g/5¹/₂ oz chilled butter,
diced

2 egg yolks

2 tbsp cold water

for the filling and topping

1 vanilla pod

400 ml/14 fl oz double cream

350 g/12 oz white chocolate,
broken into pieces

plain chocolate curls,
to decorate

cocoa powder, for dusting

white chocolate tarts

Place the flour and sugar in a bowl. Add the butter and rub it in until the mixture resembles fine breadcrumbs. Place the egg yolks and water in a separate bowl and mix together. Stir into the dry ingredients and mix to form a dough. Knead for 1 minute, or until smooth. Wrap in clingfilm and leave to chill for 20 minutes.

Preheat the oven to 200°C/400°F/Gas Mark 6. Roll out the dough on a floured work surface and use to line 12 tartlet tins. Prick the bases, cover and leave to chill for 15 minutes. Line the cases with foil and dried beans and bake for 10 minutes. Remove the beans and foil and cook for an additional 5 minutes. Leave to cool.

To make the filling, split the vanilla pod lengthways and scrape out the black seeds with a knife. Place the seeds in a saucepan with the cream and heat until almost boiling. Melt the chocolate in a heatproof bowl set over a saucepan of gently simmering water, then pour over the hot cream. Keep stirring until smooth. Whisk the mixture with an electric whisk until thickened and the whisk leaves a trail when lifted. Leave to chill in the refrigerator for 30 minutes, then whisk until soft peaks form. Divide the filling between the pastry cases and leave to chill for 30 minutes. Decorate with chocolate curls and dust with cocoa.

makes 10

for the pastry

175 g/6 oz plain flour

40 g/1¹/2 oz cocoa powder

55 g/2 oz caster sugar

pinch of salt

125 g/4¹/2 oz butter, cut into small pieces

1 egg yolk

1–2 tbsp cold water

for the sauce

200 g/7 oz blueberries

2 tbsp crème de cassis

10 g/¹/4 oz icing sugar, sifted

for the filling

140 g/5 oz plain chocolate

225 ml/8 fl oz double cream

150 ml/5 fl oz soured cream or crème fraîche

chocolate blueberry pies

To make the pastry, put the flour, cocoa, sugar and salt in a large bowl and rub in the butter until the mixture resembles breadcrumbs. Add the egg and a little cold water to form a dough. Wrap the dough and chill in the refrigerator for 30 minutes.

Remove the dough from the refrigerator and roll out. Use to line 10 x 10-cm/4-inch tartlet cases. Freeze for 30 minutes. Preheat the oven to 180°C/350°F/Gas Mark 4. Bake the cases in the oven for 15–20 minutes. Leave to cool.

Put the blueberries, cassis and icing sugar in a saucepan and warm through so that the berries become shiny but do not burst. Leave to cool.

To make the filling, melt the chocolate in a heatproof bowl set over a pan of simmering water, then cool slightly. Whip the cream until stiff and fold in the soured cream and melted chocolate.

Transfer the tartlet cases to a serving plate and divide the chocolate filling among them, smoothing the surface with a palette knife, then top with the blueberries.

makes 12

225 g/8 oz butter,
unsalted for preference,
plus extra for greasing

115 g/4 oz soft brown sugar

6 fresh apricots, halved
and stoned

115 g/4 oz plain flour

pinch of salt

1 tbsp caster sugar

1 egg yolk

1 tbsp cold water

for the chocolate sauce

115 g/4 oz plain chocolate

2 tbsp butter, unsalted
for preference

individual apricot tartes tatin

Preheat the oven to 200°C/400°F/Gas Mark 6. To make the sauce, melt the chocolate and butter together in a heatproof bowl set over a saucepan of gently simmering water and whisk until smooth. Set aside.

Grease a 12-hole muffin tin with butter, then line each hole with a disc of greaseproof paper.

Beat 140 g/5 oz of the butter with the brown sugar until very soft and divide among the holes. Place an apricot half, cut-side up, in each.

To make the pastry, place the flour and salt in a large bowl and rub in the remaining 85 g/3 oz of the butter until the mixture resembles breadcrumbs. Stir in the caster sugar. Add the egg yolk and a little cold water, if needed, to make a dough. Knead lightly and roll out. Cut out 12 x 7.5-cm/3-inch discs and fit them over the apricot halves.

Bake for 15–20 minutes, until crisp and golden. Remove from the oven and leave to stand for 5 minutes. Turn out, with the apricot on top, and drizzle with the chocolate sauce to serve.

makes 16

for the pastry

450 g/1 lb plain flour

4 tbsp lard

4 tbsp unsalted butter

125 ml/4 fl oz water

1 egg yolk, beaten, for glazing

for the filling

2 large bananas, peeled

75 g/2³/4 oz finely chopped
no-soak dried apricots

pinch of nutmeg

dash of orange juice

icing sugar, for dusting

cream or ice cream, to serve

banana pastries

To make the pastry, sift the flour into a large bowl. Add the lard and butter and rub into the flour with your fingertips until the mixture resembles breadcrumbs. Gradually blend in the water to form a soft dough. Wrap in clingfilm and leave to chill in the refrigerator for 30 minutes.

Preheat the oven to 180°C/350°F/Gas Mark 4. Mash the bananas in a bowl with a fork and stir in the apricots, nutmeg and orange juice, mixing well.

Roll the dough out on a lightly floured work surface and cut out 16 rounds, each 10 cm/4 inches in diameter.

Spoon a little of the banana filling onto one half of each round and fold the dough over the filling to make semi-circles. Pinch the edges together and seal by pressing with the prongs of a fork. Arrange the pastries on a non-stick baking tray and brush them with the beaten egg yolk. Cut a small slit in each pastry and bake in the preheated oven for 25 minutes, or until golden brown and crisp. Dust the banana pastries with icing sugar and serve hot with cream or ice cream.

makes 12

for the pastry

100 g/3¹/2 oz cold butter, cut into pieces, plus extra for greasing

225 g/8 oz plain flour, plus extra for dusting

pinch of salt

2 tsp poppy seeds

cold water

for the filling

36 cherry tomatoes

1 tbsp olive oil

25 g/1 oz unsalted butter

25 g/1 oz plain flour

270 ml/9 fl oz milk

salt and pepper

50 g/1³/4 oz mature Cheddar cheese

100 g/3¹/2 oz cream cheese

12 fresh basil leaves

cherry tomato & poppy seed tartlets

Lightly butter a 7.5-cm/3-inch, 12-hole muffin tray. Sift the flour and salt into a food processor, add the butter and process until the mixture resembles fine breadcrumbs. Tip the mixture into a large bowl and add the poppy seeds and a little cold water, just enough to bring the dough together. Turn out onto a floured surface and cut the dough in half. Roll out the first piece and cut out 6 x 9-cm/3¹/2-inch circles. Take each circle and roll out to 12 cm/4¹/2 inches in diameter and fit into the muffin holes, pressing to fill the holes. Do the same with the remaining dough. Put a piece of baking paper in each hole and fill with baking beans then put the tray in the refrigerator to chill for 30 minutes. Meanwhile, preheat the oven to 200°C/400°F/Gas Mark 6.

Remove the muffin tray from the refrigerator and bake the tartlets blind for 10 minutes in the preheated oven, then carefully remove the paper and beans. Put the tomatoes in an oven tray, drizzle with the olive oil, and roast for 5 minutes.

Melt the butter in a saucepan, stir in the flour and cook for 5–8 minutes. Gradually add the milk, stirring to combine into a white sauce. Cook for a further 5 minutes. Season well with salt and pepper and stir in the cheeses until well combined. Divide the cheese sauce among the tart cases and top with the cherry tomatoes, then put back in the oven for 15 minutes. Remove from the oven and top each tartlet with a basil leaf.

makes 6

for the pastry

70 g/2½ oz cold butter, cut into pieces, plus extra for greasing

125 g/4½ oz plain flour, plus extra for dusting

pinch of salt

cold water

for the filling

120 ml/4 fl oz crème fraîche

1 tsp creamed horseradish

½ tsp lemon juice

1 tsp Spanish capers, chopped

salt and pepper

3 egg yolks

200 g/7 oz smoked salmon trimmings

bunch of fresh dill, chopped, plus extra sprigs to garnish

smoked salmon, dill & horseradish tartlets

Butter 6 x 9-cm/3½-inch loose-bottomed fluted tart tins. Sift the flour and salt into a food processor, add the butter and process until the mixture resembles fine breadcrumbs. Tip the mixture into a large bowl and add a little cold water, just enough to bring the dough together. Turn out onto a floured surface and divide into 6 equal-sized pieces. Roll each piece to fit the tart tins. Carefully fit each piece of pastry in its case and press well to fit the tin. Roll the rolling pin over the tin to neaten the edges and trim the excess pastry. Cut 6 pieces of baking paper and fit a piece into each tart, fill with baking beans and chill in the refrigerator for 30 minutes. Meanwhile, preheat the oven to 200°C/400°F/Gas Mark 6.

Bake the tart cases for 10 minutes in the preheated oven then remove the beans and baking paper.

Meanwhile, put the crème fraîche, horseradish, lemon juice, capers and salt and pepper into a bowl and mix well. Add the egg yolks, the smoked salmon and the dill and carefully mix again. Divide this mixture among the tart cases and return to the oven for 10 minutes. Cool in the tins for 5 minutes before serving, garnished with sprigs of dill.